MY UNICORN AND ME

My Thoughts, My Dreams, My Magical Friend

STERLING CHILDREN'S BOOKS

New York

Written by Ellen Bailey and Becca Wright
Illustrated by Felicity French

For Isla May and Bronte

STERLING CHILDREN'S BOOKS
New York

An Imprint of Sterling Publishing Co., Inc.
1166 Avenue of the Americas
New York, NY 10036

ISBN 978-1-4549-3871-2

For information about custom editions, special sales, and premium and corporate purchases, please contact Sterling Special Sales at 800-805-5489 or specialsales@sterlingpublishing.com.

Manufactured in Canada

Lot #:
2 4 6 8 10 9 7 5 3
03/20

sterlingpublishing.com

Edited by Helen Brown
Designed by Derrian Bradder
Cover design by Angie Allison

Contents

Getting Started

There's nothing quite like the special bond that you have with your unicorn – it's full of magic and adventure. This book has been created for you to record all the important things that you share together. Inside, you'll find quizzes, flow charts, and stories to answer, fill in and dream about. There's space for you to write all about you and your unicorn so you can look back and remember everything in years to come.

You don't have to complete this book in any particular order – just look at the contents page and find an activity that fits your mood. Some pages have space for you to fill in the exact date, time and place, so you'll never forget exactly where you were when you completed a section. There are pages with magical quotes to inspire you, pages where you can learn how to draw a unicorn, and pictures you can color in to really make your magical mark.

This book is all about fun and friendship – just like your unicorn BFF. Enjoy!

This book was completed by

....

All About Me ...

Fill in the fact file about you below.

Date: .... Time: .... Place: ....

My name is ....

My nickname is ....

My birthday is on ....

Right now I'm .... years .... months and .... days old

The place I was born is called ....

My star sign is ....

The members of my family are ....

....

....

My best friend is called ....

My school is called ....

I have .... pet(s) called ....

My favorite color is ....

Signed ....

... And My Unicorn

Fill in the fact file about your unicorn below.

Date: .... Time: .... Place: ....

My unicorn's name is ....

My unicorn's gender is ....

My unicorn's birthday is on ....

My unicorn's star sign is ....

The color of my unicorn's coat is ....

The color of my unicorn's mane is ....

The color of my unicorn's horn is ....

My unicorn's special markings are ....

My unicorn's favorite food is ....

The place I met my unicorn was ....

My unicorn lives ....

What makes my unicorn special is ....

I love my unicorn because ....

Signed ....

This Is Us

Draw a picture of yourself on the canvas below. Why not draw yourself wearing your favorite outfit, with all of your favorite accessories?

Draw a picture of your unicorn BFF on the canvas. Don't forget to include any special markings your unicorn has — or any matching accessories.

Would You Rather?

Read each of the magical choices below and
make a decision. Would you rather ...

be invited to a unicorn's
birthday party? ☐ **OR** be invited to a
unicorn's sleepover? ☐

have three miniature unicorns
to keep in your bedroom? ☐ **OR** have one big unicorn to
keep in your garden? ☐

swim with a unicorn
in a lake? ☐ **OR** swim with a unicorn
in the ocean? ☐

trail glitter as you dance? ☐ **OR** make rainbows as you sing? ☐

have a horn that can
grant wishes? ☐ **OR** have wings that let you fly? ☐

turn into a unicorn each night
when the sun is down? ☐ **OR** turn into a unicorn each day
when the sun is up? ☐

visit a unicorn in a
castle in the clouds? ☐ **OR** visit a unicorn in an
underwater palace? ☐

meet a unicorn who
can dance? ☐ **OR** meet a unicorn who
tells jokes? ☐

have a magical instrument that attracts unicorns?	☐	OR	be able to understand and speak to unicorns? ☐
dream about unicorns every night?	☐	OR	have all the unicorns in the world dream about you? ☐
have the unicorn's power to heal the sick?	☐	OR	have the unicorn's power to see into the future? ☐
have sparkly hair?	☐	OR	have rainbow hair? ☐
take care of a unicorn and have it as a pet?	☐	OR	let it be free in the wild and visit it? ☐
ride on a unicorn's back along a beach?	☐	OR	fly next to a unicorn in the sky? ☐
have a baby unicorn to take care of?	☐	OR	have a grown-up unicorn to take care of you? ☐
be really good at drawing unicorns?	☐	OR	be really good at making up unicorn stories? ☐

Who Is Your Unicorn Sidekick?

What is your adventuring motto?

Someone who is honest, kind, and you can be completely yourself around.

A unique, hand-painted clip for its mane that totally reflects its personality.

What present would you most like to give your unicorn sidekick?

Start here

What are the most important qualities you look for in a friend?

A garland of freshly picked flowers to wear around its neck.

You meet a friend who's feeling worried. What do you do?

Where would you most like to go with your unicorn sidekick?

A beautiful meadow where you can relax in nature.

Someone who makes you laugh and you can have fun with.

It's a friend's birthday. How do you help them celebrate?

A sunny beach with waves to play in.

Be a unicorn in
a field of horses.

Stardust the Night Unicorn

Together, you and Stardust will blaze a trail. You both love to take the lead and show people how to sparkle.

Believe in magic ...
and yourself.

Crystal the Waterfall Unicorn

Like a pure waterfall, you know how to clear your mind and be at peace. For you and Crystal, calm, happy days are the name of the game.

Lie back, relax,
and take some deep
breaths together.

Talk it over and help
them see that every
day may not be good
but there's something
good in every day.

Skylark the Rainbow Unicorn

You and Skylark make a great team. You're both sensitive and optimistic, and know that every cloud has a silver lining. With the two of you around, even the darkest days will be full of color.

Organize a special day
out for the two of you
(and your two unicorn
sidekicks) full of all
their favorite things.

Sandy the Beach Unicorn

You're a fun-loving adventurer and if there's a unicorn who knows how to enjoy herself, it's Sandy! Beach party, anyone?

Call all the unicorns
and your friends
together for a huge
celebration!

Dear Unicorn

Everyone knows that unicorns are kind, and your unicorn is always willing to listen to your worries — about life, about school, about friends, or family. Use the space below to write a letter to your unicorn about anything that is on your mind.

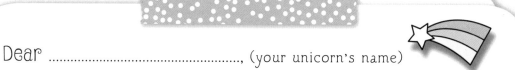

Dear ...., (your unicorn's name)

Love from, ... (your name)

Draw a Unicorn

Follow the step-by-step instructions below. Each step shows the new details to add in pink, and the final step shows what the unicorn will look like when it's finished. Use a pencil to start with, and when you are happy, go over your line in pen. Why not color in your finished unicorn?

Top Ten of Me ...

Use the space below to write down the top ten best things about yourself.
Are you a kind and caring person? Do you have an amazing imagination?
This is the place to record all of your favorite things about you.

1. ....

2. ....

3. ....

4. ....

5. ....

6. ....

7. ....

8. ....

9. ....

10. ....

... And My Unicorn

Use the space below to write down the top ten best things about your unicorn. Does your unicorn's horn sparkle in the sunshine? Are they there when you need them? This is the place to record all of your favorite things about your unicorn.

1. ....

2. ....

3. ....

4. ....

5. ....

6. ....

7. ....

8. ....

9. ....

10. ....

Unicorn A-Z

Can you think of something amazing about your unicorn for every letter of the alphabet? U is for Unicorn, of course!

A is for ....

B is for ....

C is for ....

D is for ....

E is for ....

F is for ....

G is for ....

H is for ....

I is for ....

J is for ....

K is for ....

L is for ....

M is for ....

N is for ....

O is for ....

P is for ....

Q is for ....

R is for ....

S is for ....

T is for ....

U is for ....

V is for ....

W is for ....

X is for ....

Y is for ....

Z is for ....

Ultimate Unicorn Powers

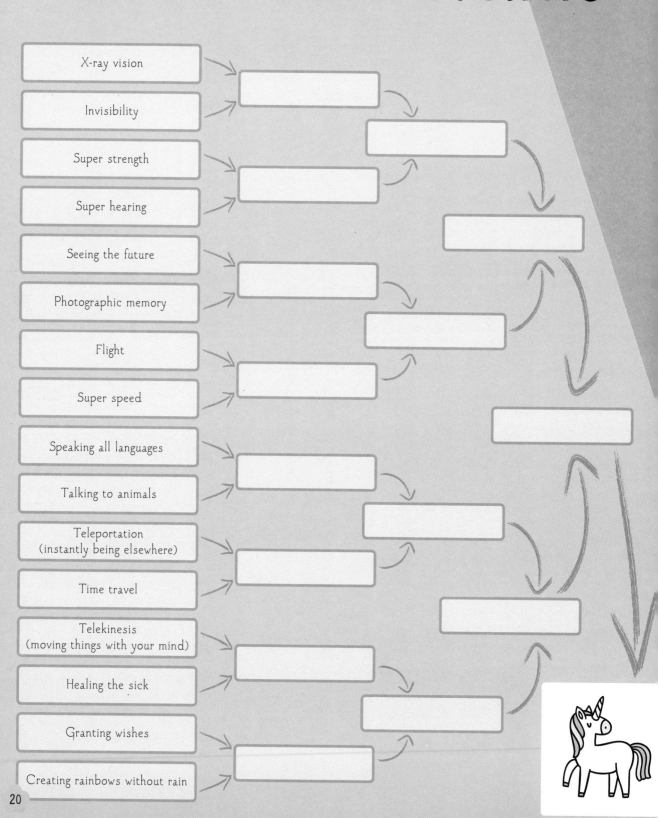

- X-ray vision
- Invisibility
- Super strength
- Super hearing
- Seeing the future
- Photographic memory
- Flight
- Super speed
- Speaking all languages
- Talking to animals
- Teleportation (instantly being elsewhere)
- Time travel
- Telekinesis (moving things with your mind)
- Healing the sick
- Granting wishes
- Creating rainbows without rain

Below are 32 unicorn powers arranged in pairs. If you had to pick one from each pair, which would you choose? Write your answers in the spaces provided, and keep choosing until you have just one left. This is your ultimate unicorn power.

Immortality
(staying alive forever)

Breathing under water

Microscopic vision
(seeing things that are tiny)

Telescopic vision
(seeing things that are far away)

Dancing glitter

Singing rainbows

Shapeshifting
(changing what you look like)

Levitation
(hovering in the air)

Telepathy
(reading minds)

Stopping time

Super flexibility

Super patience

Invulnerability
(never being injured)

Super intelligence

Night vision

Controlling the weather

My unicorn power is:

....

....

21

Draw a Unicorn

Follow the step-by-step instructions below. Each step shows the new details to add in pink, and the final step shows what the unicorn will look like when it's finished. Use a pencil to start with, and when you are happy, go over your line in pen. Why not color in your finished unicorn?

Let
ME BE YOUR
Rainbow

What's Your Unicorn Style?

Every unicorn has its own personal style. Take this quiz and then turn over to page 26 to find out your personal style.

1. You and your unicorn are going to spend the afternoon together. What do you do?
   a. Pick some flowers to make a daisy chain
   b. Paint pictures of each other
   c. Practice your dance moves

2. What would your dream bedroom be like?
a. A floaty, calm space with fairy lights and a canopy over the bed
b. A bright, fun bedroom with a climbing wall and colorful bedspread
   c. Sequins everywhere and a stage area for performances

3. What's your favorite thing about going to school?
   a. Reading and writing stories
   b. Sports – I love playing games with my friends
   c. Being part of the school play

4. Your unicorn offers to take you for a ride on its back. Where do you go?
   a. Galloping through a beautiful meadow
   b. Splashing through waves on a beach
   c. To a unicorn party

5. It's your unicorn's birthday. What kind of cake do you bake?

a. A vanilla sponge cake decorated with sugar roses

b. A rainbow cake with multicolored layers

c. A chocolate cake covered in edible glitter

6. You're playing hairdressers with your unicorn. How do you style its mane?

a. Weave flowers through its hair

b. Use hair chalk to add multicolored stripes

c. Add feathers and jewels to glam it up

7. Your teacher says you can decorate your homework book however you like. What do you do?

a. Draw an intricate pattern of swirls, hearts, and unicorns

b. Cut pictures of unicorns out of magazines and stick them all over to make a collage

c. Stick on plenty of jewels and sparkly stickers

8. You're going for a sleepover with your unicorn. What's the most important item in your suitcase?

a. A friendship bracelet you've made for your unicorn

b. Cookies you've baked for a midnight feast

c. A microphone for a singing competition

Mostly "a"s – perfect pastels

You're calm and thoughtful. You feel you're most happy and relaxed in nature. Soft, springtime colors are a perfect match for you. Think of pale green shoots poking through the ground, pink blossom on the trees, and fluffy yellow ducks that have just hatched. Why not try wearing pastel shades today and see how it makes you feel?

Mostly "b"s – vibrant rainbow

You're full of energy and love to have fun. You're bright and bold, just like a rainbow. Color-blocking is a fashion style where you wear big blocks of bright color all together – maybe a red T-shirt, a purple cardigan, and yellow pants. Ditch the dark blues, blacks, and grays, and see how many different rainbow colors you can get into your outfit today.

Mostly "c"s – glittery glam

You're a confident party person who loves to be the center of attention. You feel your best when your outfit sparkles like a diamond. The secret of glittery glam style is to start with neutral colors such as white, gray, cream, and black. Next, add some sparkle with sequins, mirrors, and metallics. Experiment with adding jewel colors such as emerald green, ruby red, and sapphire blue to your outfits to really make them pop.

Color me beautiful

Would You Rather?

The Holiday Unicorn has invited you for a day out. Read each of the magical choices below and make a decision. Would you rather ...

share a breakfast of happy pancakes? ☐ **OR** share a breakfast of dreams on toast? ☐

wear something floaty and relaxed? ☐ **OR** wear something sparkling and stylish? ☐

chill at home for a while? ☐ **OR** head straight out? ☐

travel over a rainbow? ☐ **OR** travel under the sea? ☐

arrive at a beautiful beach? ☐ **OR** arrive at a wonderful woodland? ☐

meet up with friends? ☐ **OR** be just the two of you? ☐

visit a land made of sweets? ☐ **OR** visit a magical futuristic city? ☐

build a den? ☐ **OR** build a sandcastle? ☐

swim under a waterfall?	☐	**OR**	play in the clouds? ☐
snack on fairy cake pops?	☐	**OR**	snack on enchanted ice cream? ☐
go on a treasure hunt?	☐	**OR**	make wishes on dandelions? ☐
eat at a fairy feast?	☐	**OR**	eat at a butterfly banquet? ☐
make a crown of flowers?	☐	**OR**	make a necklace of shells? ☐
sing songs around a campfire?	☐	**OR**	dance around a fairy ring? ☐
travel home at sunset?	☐	**OR**	stay out until midnight? ☐
stay up telling fairy stories?	☐	**OR**	sleep and dream of unicorns? ☐

What Would Your Unicorn Do?

Unicorns have three ways of making things right: using their magical powers, coming up with a fun idea, or using their wisdom. Read through each of the problems below and circle which of the three ways you think your unicorn would choose to solve it.

You and your unicorn are off for a day at the beach, but you can't find your towel. What happens next?

Magic: Your unicorn uses its X-ray vision to scan your home and finds the towel.

Fun: Did you know that unicorns can use their horns to weave material? New towel coming up!

Wisdom: Your unicorn questions you about where you last saw the towel and uses your answers to track it down.

Oh no! It's a hot summer day and your ice cream has melted. How does your unicorn get you out of this sticky mess?

Magic: It refreezes your treat with its ice powers.

Fun: It uses its horn to stir it into a delicious milkshake.

Wisdom: It gives you a hug and tells you it's fine to be disappointed – it'll still be a great day.

The smoke alarm has gone off. The chocolate cake you've made has burnt in the oven . . . how does your unicorn save the day?

Magic: It reverses time so that you can go back and get the cake out of the oven before it burns.

Fun: The cake might be burnt, but that doesn't mean you can't have a food fight with it.

Wisdom: Your unicorn suggests you chop off the burnt parts and use a cookie cutter to make mini cakes from the middle. If you cover them with icing, no one will notice – yum!

Two of your friends have had an argument. They're asking you to choose which one of them you're going to play with. How does your unicorn help you solve this tricky friendship dilemma?

Magic: It uses its powers to wipe your friends' memories of the argument.

Fun: Your unicorn suggests you all play a game of find-the-unicorn. It's so much fun, your friends are prepared to put their argument to one side so that you can all play it together.

Wisdom: It explains to your friends that they are making you unhappy and helps them make up.

You're halfway to school when you realize you've forgotten your sports clothes. Your teacher gets annoyed when people are late. Luckily, you've got your unicorn to help you out . . . what does it do?

Magic: It uses its powers to summon your sports clothes – they'll be in your locker when you get to school.

Fun: You hop onto its back and gallop back home to get it, so you still arrive on time. Yee-haw!

Wisdom: Your unicorn encourages you to face your teacher. You apologize for being late and offer to help with a classroom task during the day to make up for it.

You've spent ages making a birthday card for a friend when your scissors slip and the card is cut in two. How does your unicorn make things right?

Magic: It touches its horn to the cut to make the card magically fix itself back together.

Fun: It chops the card up into even more pieces and uses them to create a collage on a new card.

Wisdom: It helps you make it into a special friendship card – your friend keeps one half and you keep the other, and when the two of you are together, the card's complete.

Your friends want you to go to the park with them but your mom says you can't go until your bedroom is tidy. Unicorn to the rescue! But how?

Magic: Your unicorn uses their super-speed power to help you get the tidying done in no time at all.

Fun: Your unicorn puts some music on and you both dance around while you tidy up – you have so much fun that you don't mind getting to the park a bit late.

Wisdom: Your unicorn suggests you make a deal with your mom: you'll do half the tidying now and half when you get back from the park.

You're about to go on a camping trip when it starts raining. Should you give up and go home? No! You've got a unicorn to help . . . but how?

Magic: It uses its powers to control the weather and make it sunny.

Fun: You both dance in the rain and play in the mud.

Wisdom: Your unicorn helps you make a list of things you can do in the tent while listening to the sound of the rain. Together you have a wonderful time swapping stories, telling jokes, and making perfect plans for the next sunny day.

Unicorn Elements

Look at the unicorns below, one for each of the four elements — water, fire, earth, and air. What powers do you think each unicorn would have? Circle your favorite idea for each and then color in the unicorns.

Water

Breathing under water

Shapeshifting (changing into different kinds of animal)

Foresight (seeing what will happen in the future)

Fire

Super strength

Super speed

Time travel

Earth

Healing

Immortality
(living forever)

X-ray vision

Air

Flight

Invisibility

Telepathy
(reading minds)

Birthday Unicorns

For each month of the year there's a birthday unicorn.
Find out which yours is and see if your personality matches theirs.
Wear your birthday unicorn's color to harness their power.

January – Garnet Unicorn

Birthstone:
Garnet
Personality:
Brave and full of energy
Power:
Keeps travelers safe. If ever you're going
on a long journey, the Garnet Unicorn can
use its powers to protect you from harm.

February – Amethyst Unicorn

Birthstone:
Amethyst
Personality:
Calm and organized
Power:
Gives you courage. Feeling nervous
about something? The Amethyst
Unicorn can help you feel brave
and face your fears.

March – Aquamarine Unicorn

Birthstone:
Aquamarine
Personality:
Creative and trustworthy
Power:
Protects against ocean dangers.
The Aquamarine Unicorn loves water
and watches over you when you
go in the sea.

April – Diamond Unicorn

Birthstone:
Diamond
Personality:
Dependable and fun
Power:
Brings you love. The Diamond Unicorn enjoys filling people's lives with sparkles, magic, and true love.

May – Emerald Unicorn

Birthstone:
Emerald
Personality:
Loving and relaxed
Power:
Brings you wisdom. Need help figuring out a tricky problem? The Emerald Unicorn can save the day.

June – Pearl Unicorn

Birthstone:
Pearl
Personality:
Elegant and helpful
Power:
Makes you graceful. Want to move with the elegance of a ballerina? The Pearl Unicorn can help you out.

July – Ruby Unicorn

Birthstone:
Ruby
Personality:
Loving and strong
Power:
Protects you from evil.
Need rescuing from a bad situation?
The Ruby Unicorn can keep you safe.

August – Peridot Unicorn

Birthstone:
Peridot
Personality:
Confident and daring
Power:
Stops you from having nightmares.
The Peridot Unicorn uses its powers
to make sure all your dreams are
full of joy and happiness.

September – Sapphire Unicorn

Birthstone:
Sapphire
Personality:
Wise and honest
Power:
Keeps you healthy. The Sapphire
Unicorn can protect you from
coughs and sneezes, and help you
feel ready to take on every day.

October – Opal Unicorn

Birthstone:
Opal
Personality:
Happy and energetic
Power:
Brings hope. If ever you're feeling down in the dumps, the Opal Unicorn can help you look on the bright side.

November – Topaz Unicorn

Birthstone:
Topaz
Personality:
Wise and brave
Power:
Makes you strong. Even the smallest person can feel powerful with the help of the Topaz Unicorn.

December – Turquoise Unicorn

Birthstone:
Turquoise
Personality:
Loving and lucky
Power:
Brings good fortune. If ever you have a run of bad luck, the Turquoise Unicorn can turn things around and make good things happen for you.

Unicorn Wishes

While out exploring, you've come across a rare kind of unicorn that can grant wishes, and it has agreed to grant you three. What do you wish for?

Wish 1:

....
....
....

Wish 2:

....
....
....

Wish 3:

....
....
....

Draw a Unicorn

Follow the step-by-step instructions below. Each step shows the new details to add in pink, and the final step shows what the unicorn will look like when it's finished. Use a pencil to start with, and when you are happy, go over your line in pen. Why not color in your finished unicorn?

A Perfect Day

Imagine you and your unicorn are going to spend a perfect day together.
What do you think would happen? Fill in the gaps in the story below to find out.
You can use the ideas in brackets to help you, or make it up as you go along.
Whatever you end up doing, make sure your day is full of sparkles.

It's 7am and you're woken up by a unicorn nuzzling your cheek. "Good
morning, ... (your favorite unicorn name),"
you exclaim. The unicorn is all the colors of the rainbow and has a beautiful
pattern of .... (hearts / diamonds / flowers)
on its back. "I've planned a special day out for you!" says the unicorn. You are
so excited and can't wait to get started.

You dress in your favorite outfit, which is ....
....
(jeans and a T-shirt / a dress / your snuggly rainbow onesie), then eat a delicious
breakfast of ....
(pancakes / cereal / toast). As you take the last bite, the doorbell rings.
You answer it and are surprised to see ....
and .... (names of your two best friends).
"I invited them to join us," says the unicorn. You give your best friends a big
hug – you are so excited that you all get to spend the day together.

"Hop onto my back," says the unicorn. "We're off to the land of rainbows."
Suddenly, the room fills with ....
(mist / glitter / colored light) and *whoosh*! The air clears and you see that you're
now in a magical rainbow land. "Which color do you want to explore first?"

asks the unicorn. "..,"
(Red / Orange / Yellow / Green / Blue / Indigo / Violet) you and your best friends
all exclaim at the same time. The unicorn leads the way and you're amazed to
find that even the air smells of ....
(a fruit that's the color of the rainbow you've chosen). There's a table piled with
.... and ....
(toys / art materials / clothes that are that color), and you and your best friends
have a fantastic time playing with everything.

You spend the day exploring all the different colors. Each color has a different
mood, and your favorite is ....
(your favorite color), which makes you feel ....
(happy / relaxed / creative). In each color you meet a ....
(fairy / elf / mermaid) who gives you and each of your best friends a beautiful
bead. At the end of the day you have a bead of every color. The unicorn shows
you how to make them into a rainbow ....
(necklace / friendship bracelet / hair accessory).

"It's time for us to go home now," says the unicorn, "but if ever you want to
come back here, just touch each bead and say "..
(its color / the unicorn's name / a magical word)."

You and your best friends look at each other in amazement. "Let's come back
again ....
(tomorrow / next week / on my birthday)," you suggest, and you all pinky promise
that you will.

A Perfect Night

There's only one thing that's more exciting than a perfect unicorn day, and that's a perfect unicorn night. Imagine if instead of going to bed one evening, you got to go on an adventure with your unicorn while everyone else was asleep. What would you do? Fill in the gaps in the story below to find out. You can use the ideas in brackets to help you, or make it up as you go along.

It's late in the evening. You've brushed your teeth and you've climbed into bed, but this is no time for sleeping! You throw back the covers and jump up, wearing ....
(your pajamas / your dance clothes / your favorite outfit) and open your wardrobe door. Hiding inside is a unicorn. "Hello ....
(your favorite unicorn name)," you say. "What shall we do tonight?"

"We're going on a journey using ....
(my wings / a magical rainbow / fairy dust)," says the unicorn. "Quick, open the window and jump on my back." You do as the unicorn asks, and in a flash of sparkling light you're whisked up into the night sky. Soon you're flying up high, and you can see ....
(lights on in the houses below / the full moon / stars twinkling in the sky). "Let's stop for a midnight feast," suggests the unicorn. You land on ....
....
(the top of a mountain / the roof of a grand palace / a moonlit beach), and the unicorn gets out a feast of ....
(chocolate / cake / fruit). When you've had enough to eat, you set off again into the night.

"We're going on a dream hunt" says the unicorn. "Let's find some wonderful

dreams and take them back for ....
(the person you would like to give a dream to)." You soon arrive in the Land of Dreams, and the unicorn gives you a special silver bag. In the distance you spot a ....
(sparkling shell / glowing flower / gleaming pebble). "That's a dream," exclaims the unicorn, "go and get it." You run to the dream and catch it in the bag. Together, you and the unicorn fill dozens of silver bags with dreams. "That was amazing!" you shout, feeling tired but happy.

You jump on the unicorn's back and fly home just as the sun begins to rise. As you pass over the house of ....
(the person you would like to give a dream to) you open one of the silver bags and throw the dream down to them. The dream knows exactly where to go and what to do, and soon they're dreaming of ....
....
....
....
....
(the dream you've given them).

The unicorn takes you back to your own bed and tucks you in. Just as you're dozing off, the unicorn opens another one of the silver bags, and you begin to dream of ....
....
....
....
(a dream you'd love to have). What a magical night!

SPARKLE WHEREVER *you* GO

The Unicorn Alphabet

Have you ever wondered how unicorns communicate with each other?
They have their own magical language, which has its own special
unicorn alphabet. It's perfect for writing with a horn or a hoof,
but you could use a pen or pencil, too.

A	♠	J	Σ	S	◇
B	♦	K	~	T	◐
C	↑	L	✳	U	★
D	☺	M	⌐	V	♥
E	☽	N	→	W	○
F	▷	O	⊗	X	⚡
G	■	P	⊡	Y	»
H	Γ	Q	⋈	Z	⁸⁸
I	△	R	⌂		

Use the empty space below to practice writing out the unicorn alphabet.

Write these sentences below in the unicorn alphabet.

I love unicorns: ....

....

Unicorns love me: ....

....

Use the unicorn alphabet to fill in the sentences below.

My name is spelled ....

.... in the unicorn alphabet.

My unicorn's name is spelled ....

.... in the unicorn alphabet.

My best friend's name is spelled ....

.... in the unicorn alphabet.

Unicorn Poetry

Poetry is a great way to express your feelings.
Using the letters U, N, I, C, O, R, N, S to begin the first word of
each line, write a poem about how much you love unicorns.

U ....

N ....

I ....

C ....

O ....

R ....

N ....

S ....

Use the rhyming pairs below to
help you with your poem.

unicorn / horn	stars / Mars
fly / sky	wings / things
bright / light	cloud / proud
heart / start	flower / tower
moon / soon	gold / bold
sun / fun	shine / mine

What I Love About Me ...

Finish the sentences below with all the things you love about you.

I love that I can ....

....

I love that I am ....

....

I love that I have ....

....

I love that I do ....

....

I love that I always ....

....

I love that I am able to ....

....

I love that I look like ....

....

I love that I would never ....

....

I love that I like ....

....

... And My Unicorn

Finish the sentences below with all the things you love about your unicorn.

I love that my unicorn can ....

....

I love that my unicorn is ....

....

I love that my unicorn has ....

....

I love that my unicorn does ....

....

I love that my unicorn will always ....

....

I love that my unicorn is able to ....

....

I love that my unicorn looks like ....

....

I love that my unicorn would never ....

....

I love that my unicorn likes ....

....

The Magic Words

Create a secret spell that will summon your unicorn to your side instantly, and make sure only you know the magic words. Write the magic words below.

Draw a Unicorn

Follow the step-by-step instructions below. Each step shows the new details to add in pink, and the final step shows what the unicorn will look like when it's finished. Use a pencil to start with, and when you are happy, go over your line in pen. Why not color in your finished unicorn?

Together We Are

Unicorns know that to really shine it's important to know yourself and what your strengths are. Look at all the words below and color in any that you would use to describe **your** personality.

Brave

Strong

Powerful

Clever

Cheerful

Kind

Generous

Adventurous

Fun

Creative

Sensible

Enthusiastic

Happy

Imaginative

Organized

Intelligent

Positive

Loving

Honest

Confident

Now color in any of the words below that you would use to describe **your unicorn**. Which words have you colored in on both pages? Together, you and your unicorn are all these things!

Brave

Strong

Powerful

Clever

Cheerful

Kind

Generous

Adventurous

Fun

Creative

Sensible

Enthusiastic

Happy

Imaginative

Organized

Intelligent

Positive

Loving

Honest

Confident

Unicorn Day

Like a birthday, Unicorn Day is a massive celebration. It's a day dedicated to one thing and one thing only . . . unicorns! And the best thing about the day? Each unicorn lover gets to decide when their Unicorn Day takes place and what happens on it. Answer the questions below to plan your very own Unicorn Day.

What is the date of your Unicorn Day? ....

What kind of decorations will there be? ....

What will you eat for breakfast that morning? ....
....

What will you do to make the morning extra magical? ....
....
....

What will you wear on Unicorn Day? ....
....

How will you do your hair? ....
....

Is there anywhere special you'll go on Unicorn Day? ....
....

Will you invite friends or family to celebrate with you? ....
....

Will you make anyone a card or present? ....

....

Are you going to start any Unicorn Day traditions? ....

....

....

Will you bake something special? ....

....

What other food will you eat? ....

....

What kind of music will you listen to? ....

....

Will you make up a unicorn song, dance or poem? ....

....

What games will you play? ....

....

Which unicorn-themed bedtime story will you finish the day with?

....

What will you wear to bed? ....

....

Unicorns in the Past

Let your mind travel back through the past — what do you think unicorns used to be like? Tick the boxes next to the sentences that you think are true.

Unicorns were the first creatures on Earth. ◇

The first unicorns had multicolored zebra stripes. ◇

Unicorns used their magical powers to protect themselves from dinosaurs. ◇

Unicorns lived in caves decorated with wild flowers. ◇

Unicorns made friends with the first humans, and they lived happily together. ◇

Unicorns had sparkly, shaggy coats – a bit like glittering woolly mammoths. ◇

Unicorns taught humans how to make fires so they could cook their food. ◇

Unicorns were a symbol of freedom and power. ◇

Unicorns had short, stumpy tails. Over the years they have evolved to have beautiful, long tails. ◇

The king and queen of the unicorns held balls in their palace where they danced all night. ◇

Unicorns in the Future

Now imagine yourself in a unicorn-tastic future! What do you think it will be like? Tick the boxes next to the sentences that you think are true.

Cars will be powered by rainbow unicorn poop. ◇

There will be many more unicorns than there are today. ◇

Unicorns will stop being so shy, and we'll see them everywhere. ◇

Every human will have a unicorn best friend. ◇

Unicorns will guide us to a world full of happiness, glitter, and rainbows. ◇

Unicorns will encourage other magical creatures, such as fairies and mermaids, to reveal themselves. ◇

Unicorns will teach humans magic that makes the world a better place. ◇

Unicorns will travel into space and find other planets for us to live on. ◇

Unicorns will use their powers to heal the world and help the environment. ◇

Unicorns will start doing jobs like humans do – they'll be doctors, teachers, and even pop stars. ◇

What Is Your Spiritual Season?

What color clothes is your wardrobe full of?

Trying something new that you've never done before.

Which part of a vacation do you enjoy the most?

The journey there, feeling excited about everything that's to come.

Start here

You've got a Saturday afternoon free. How do you spend it?

The middle of the vacation when you're completely relaxed and into the swing of it.

How tidy is your bedroom?

What would be your ideal birthday party?

Playing games outside with your friends.

Practicing a new skill to get really good at it.

How would you cheer up a friend who was feeling down?

Dressing up in sequins and dancing under a disco ball.

Pastel pinks, baby blues, and pale yellows.

Spirit of Spring

Like the world waking up from a long, cold winter, you love fresh starts and new beginnings. Your spirit is full of the excitement of the beginning of the year.

Bright, bold colors of the rainbow.

Spirit of Summer

Your spirit is laid back and fun-loving. You're full of energy and enthusiasm, like a midsummer's day. Keep smiling!

Not that tidy – you have a carefree attitude to life.

Super organized – you like to know where everything is.

Spirit of Autumn

Think of a squirrel playing in fallen leaves and carefully hiding its nuts for winter. Your spirit is all about being thoughtful and wise, but also having fun. Great combination!

Listen carefully and let them know you'll always be there for them.

Spirit of Winter

Like the spirit of winter, you shine on even the darkest of days. Your loving warmth keeps everyone toasty through the cold winter months.

Make them laugh and help them to see the glitter in the gloom.

Best Unicorn Names: It's a Girl

Use the space below to write down the ten best names for a girl unicorn.

1. ....

2. ....

3. ....

4. ....

5. ....

6. ....

7. ....

8. ....

9. ....

10. ....

Best Unicorn Names: It's a Boy

Use the space below to write down the ten best names for a boy unicorn.

1. ....

2. ....

3. ....

4. ....

5. ....

6. ....

7. ....

8. ....

9. ....

10. ....

Draw a Unicorn

Follow the step-by-step instructions below. Each step shows the new details to add in pink, and the final step shows what the unicorn will look like when it's finished. Use a pencil to start with, and when you are happy, go over your line in pen. Why not color in your finished unicorn?

Our Favorite Things

Fill in the spaces below with all of you and your unicorn's favorite things — do you like all the same stuff or do you have totally different tastes?

My favorite food is ....

My unicorn's favorite food is ....

My favorite drink is ....

My unicorn's favorite drink is ....

My favorite color is ....

My unicorn's favorite color is ....

My favorite movie is ....

My unicorn's favorite movie is ....

My favorite song is ....

My unicorn's favorite song is ....

My favorite book is ....

My unicorn's favorite book is ....

My favorite game is ....

My unicorn's favorite game is ....

My favorite place is ....

My unicorn's favorite place is ....

Unicorn Fortune Finder

Have you ever wondered what the future holds for you and your unicorn?
Use this mystic fortune finder to find out.

How to make it

1. Cut around the fortune finder on the opposite page. Fold one corner over to the other to make a triangle, so that the writing is on the outside.

2. Fold your triangle in half again to form a smaller triangle. Then unfold the sheet and lie it flat, writing side down.

4. Turn the fortune finder over and repeat step **3**, folding the new corners into the middle.

5. Fold the fortune finder in half from edge to edge, so the colors remain on the outside.

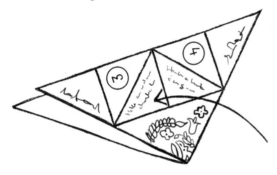

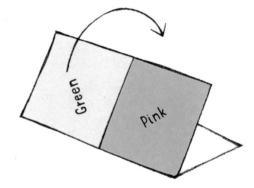

3. Fold each corner of the sheet into the middle, so the corners all meet at the center of the sheet.

6. Unfold and fold in half the other way.

7. Slide the thumb and forefinger of both hands under the flaps of the fortune finder, and find your fortune!

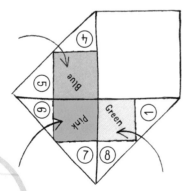

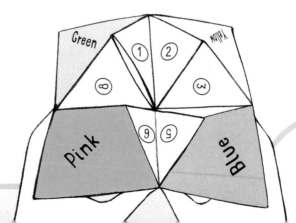

Blue

Pink

5

6

4

7

Your unicorn will
have a baby unicorn.

You will see
a rainbow.

Your unicorn's mane
may mysteriously
change color.

Your unicorn will
grant you
a wish.

You and your unicorn are
about to make an
exciting discovery.

You and your unicorn
will discover buried
treasure.

3

8

Yellow

Green

2

1

Your unicorn will
be with you forever.

You will go on a
great adventure with
your unicorn.

What to do next

Either you or a friend should pick a color from the outside flaps.
Spell out the color, opening and closing the fortune finder for each
letter. Holding the fortune finder open, ask yourself or your companion
to pick one of the numbers shown inside. Count out the number and pick
another one. Lift that number's flap to reveal a fortune on the other side.

Fill the back of your unicorn fortune finder with flowers and color them in.

What's the best cereal
for a unicorn to eat?
Uni-corn flakes.

Why does a unicorn hate school?
Because of the uni-forms.

What is a unicorn's favorite
type of bedtime story?
A fairy tail.

How do unicorns get to the park?
On a uni-cycle.

I'M A

Believer

Unicorn Quick Quiz

You totally love unicorns, but how well do you really know them?
Take this quick quiz to find out.

1. What does "uni" mean in the word "unicorn"?
a. One
b. Beloved
c. Everywhere

2. Which of the following would a unicorn be most likely to do?
a. Pull a sleigh and deliver presents
b. Use its magical powers to help you
c. Guard a pot of gold at the end of a rainbow

3. What is the real name for a unicorn horn?
a. Antler
b. Alicorn
c. Dorsal

4. What is unicorn poop like?
a. Rainbow colored
b. Smelly
c. Enormous

5. Which underwater animal has a horn like a unicorn's?
a. Narwhal
b. Seahorse
c. Shark

Answers: 1.a 2.b 3.b 4.a 5.a

The Best Parts

Unicorns make the best friends. But what are the most important things you look for in a friend? Color in the hearts of the qualities that are important to you.

A good friend ...

Keeps secrets

Makes you laugh

Shares their sweets with you

Tells the truth

Is adventurous

Is a good listener

Is fun to be around

Accepts you

Stands up for you

Is confident

Likes doing the same things as you

Is loyal

Is supportive

Is creative

Gets your jokes

Is unique

Share the Power

Imagine that every day for the next week your unicorn will share its magic power with you. What will you do? Choose from the answers in brackets to fill in the gaps, or go wild and make up your own.

Monday: Invisibility

Creep into your friends' houses and ....

(try on all their clothes / leave presents for them / fill their fridges with tasty food)

Scare your family by ....

(making it look like your teddy bear is flying in the air / disappearing from sight / making spooky noises in their ears)

Tuesday: Flight

Fly over the place you live and ....

(wave to all your friends / drop candy down / become friends with the birds)

Join your unicorn friends on a magical adventure ....

(to the Land of Unicorns / to a tropical island / to a mountain peak)

Wednesday: Telekinesis (moving objects with your mind)

Use your power to ....

(get the remote control before others / score goals to win games / give yourself extra helpings of dessert)

Be extra lazy and ....

(lift food to your mouth without using your hands / tidy your room while lying down / washing up while watching TV)

Thursday: Shapeshifting (changing what you look like)

Shift into the shape of an adult so that ....

(you don't have to go to school / you can drive a car / you can pretend to be your teacher)

Shift into the shape of an animal ....

(so that you can play with your pet / so you can run free / so you don't have to do chores)

Friday: Telepathy (mind reading)

Read your teacher's mind to ....

(discover the answers to a test / find out what they're going to say about you at parents' evening / get them their ideal end-of-year present)

Read your best friend's mind to ....

(beat them to the punchlines of all their jokes / see if they always tell the truth / find out what they really think about unicorns)

Saturday: Speak any language

Make new friends who speak different languages and ....

(amaze them with your skills / learn songs in their language / go on a trip together)

Talk to animals and ....

(chat to your pet / find out what the birds are saying / speak to the animals at the zoo)

Sunday: Time travel

Go back into the past and ....

(see what life was like before TV / dress in funny clothes / meet the first-ever unicorn)

Zoom into the future and ....

(be served by robots / see what you'll look like / meet the unicorns of the future)

Do You Believe?

Of course you believe in unicorns — but do you believe in these "mythical" creatures? Circle the ones you believe in and then color them in.

Fairies

Witches

Dragons

Mermaids

Elves

Vampires

Trolls

How Do You Say?

Have you ever wondered what unicorns are called in other countries? Here's how to say "unicorn" in ten different languages — useful if you ever find yourself in need of summoning a unicorn no matter where you are.

French:
Licorne

Korean: 일각수
(Ilgagsu)

Swahili:
Nyati

Russian: единорог
(Yedinorog)

Japanese: ユニコーン
(Yunikōn)

Chinese: 独角兽
(Dú jiǎo shòu)

German:
Einhorn

Spanish:
Unicornio

Samoan:
Laʻau

Hindi: एक तंगावाला
(Ek tangaavaala)

Unicorn Author

Imagine you are writing a book all about unicorns — what kind of book will it be? Fill out your answers below. It's sure to be a bestseller!

First things first, what kind of book is it?

☐ Picture book   ☐ Photography book   ☐ Handbook: how to care for unicorns
☐ Novel   ☐ Puzzle book   ☐ Fact book   ☐ Real-life adventure story

What will the book be called?

....

Will it have illustrations?

☐ Yes, of course   ☐ No, this is a very serious book

Who will read it?

☐ Children   ☐ Adults   ☐ Anyone who believes in unicorns

How long will it be?

☐ A short book that you can fit in your pocket and take with you everywhere
☐ A big, long book that's packed with unicorn facts and information

Write a little bit about your book below:

....

....

....

Cover Design

It's time to design a cover for your unicorn book. How will you make people want to pick up your book? Draw and color in your ideal cover below. Don't forget to put your name on it.

A Week Full of Unicorns

If you could have a week off school and just fill it with unicorn-themed activities, what would your perfect week look like? Would you go searching for unicorns with your best friend? Maybe you'd throw a glittery unicorn party, or bake a rainbow cake fit for a unicorn? Whatever you decide to do, don't forget to have fun.

Monday

What will you do? ....

How long will it take? ....

Where will it take place? ....

What will you need? ....

Will you be doing it alone or with a friend? ....

What will you wear? ....

☆

Tuesday

What will you do? ....

How long will it take? ....

Where will it take place? ....

What will you need? ....

Will you be doing it alone or with a friend? ....

What will you wear? ....

☆

Wednesday

What will you do? ....

How long will it take? ....

Where will it take place? ....

What will you need? ....

Will you be doing it alone or with a friend? ....

What will you wear? ....

Thursday

What will you do? ....

How long will it take? ....

Where will it take place? ....

What will you need? ....

Will you be doing it alone or with a friend? ....

What will you wear? ....

☆

Friday

What will you do? ....

How long will it take? ....

Where will it take place? ....

What will you need? ....

Will you be doing it alone or with a friend? ....

What will you wear? ....

☆

Saturday

What will you do? ....

How long will it take? ....

Where will it take place? ....

What will you need? ....

Will you be doing it alone or with a friend? ....

What will you wear? ....

☆

Sunday

What will you do? ....

How long will it take? ....

Where will it take place? ....

What will you need? ....

Will you be doing it alone or with a friend? ....

What will you wear? ....

Ultimate Sugar Rush

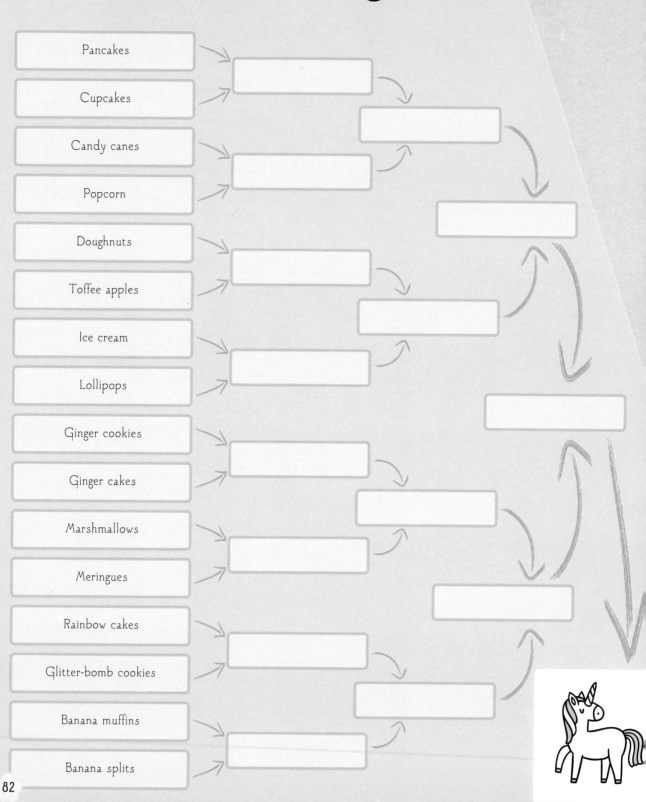

Pancakes

Cupcakes

Candy canes

Popcorn

Doughnuts

Toffee apples

Ice cream

Lollipops

Ginger cookies

Ginger cakes

Marshmallows

Meringues

Rainbow cakes

Glitter-bomb cookies

Banana muffins

Banana splits

What is your ultimate unicorn sweet treat? Below are 32 tasty treats that unicorns love, arranged in pairs. If you had to pick one from each pair, which would you choose? Write your answers in the spaces provided, and keep choosing until you have just one left. This is your ultimate unicorn sugar rush.

Chocolate milkshakes

Chocolate sundaes

Cake pops

Popsicles

Strawberry cookies

Strawberry candy

Fudge

Hot chocolate with whipped cream

Brownies

Ice cream sandwiches

Cheesecake

Caramel shortbread

Scones

Pie

Eclairs

Macarons

My unicorn sugar rush is:

....

....

Best Unicorn Games

Unicorns love to play games. Rank the games below from one to ten in the order you'd most like to play them with your unicorn BFF.

Marbles

Hopscotch

Apple bobbing

Hide-and-seek

Hula hooping

Tag

Skipping

Simon says

Musical chairs

Monkey in the middle

1. ....

2. ....

3. ....

4. ....

5. ....

6. ....

7. ....

8. ....

9. ....

10. ....

Draw-a-corn

Put your imagination to the test. Read the descriptions of unicorns below and use the information to draw pictures of what you think they might look like.

Bloom

Where it comes from:
Holland
Interesting features:
Has flowers woven into its mane
Special power:
Can make flowers blossom in its path

Starburst

Where it comes from:
Sirius - the brightest star in our sky
Interesting features:
Has a pattern of stars on its back
Special power:
Its horn glows to light up the night

Icicle

Where it comes from:
North Pole
Interesting features:
Has a horn that is an icicle
Special power:
Can turn anything to snow or ice

Orbit

Where it comes from:
Saturn's rings in our solar system
Interesting features:
Has beautiful yellow stripes around its body
Special power:
Can slow down time

Sea Breeze

Where it comes from:
Hawaii
Interesting features:
Has a wavy tail as blue as the ocean
Special power:
Can breathe under water

Twilight

Where it comes from:
India
Interesting features:
Glows like a sunset at dusk
Special power:
Invisibility

Flutterby

Where it comes from:
Mexico
Interesting features:
Is always surrounded by butterflies
Special power:
Can talk to all animals

Dancer

Where it comes from:
Kenya
Interesting features:
Has sparkly, silver hooves
Special power:
Super speed

Fly, Fly Away

Lucky you! You're the guest of a flying unicorn for the day — one of the rarest kinds of unicorn — and you can go wherever you like. What adventures will you have and what places will you explore?

What color are the flying unicorn's wings?

White   Pink   Blue   Purple   Rainbow

What color is the flying unicorn's horn?

Red   Green   Silver   Gold   Yellow

Which three places would you like to visit on the flying unicorn? Write them below.

1. ....
2. ....
3. ....

With the flying unicorn, which places will you explore?

Mountains   Oceans   Cities   Deserts   Rainforests

What mythical creature would you most like the flying unicorn to take you to see?

A mermaid   A fairy   An elf   A pixie   A troll

What adventure are you most excited about having with the flying unicorn? Write about it in the space below.

....
....
....
....
....
....

What activity are you most excited about doing with the flying unicorn? Write about it in the space below.

....
....
....
....
....
....

Award Ceremony

Imagine you're the host of a glittering award ceremony and you have eight prizes to give out. Read the descriptions of the unicorns opposite and decide which unicorn should win which award.

Most energetic

Most stylish

Most mysterious

Most shy

Most adventurous

Most wise

Most likely to make you laugh

Most likely to help a friend

Chipper

Always ready to cheer you up when you're feeling down, this happy unicorn is full of fun and laughter. Chipper always dresses smartly but isn't afraid of looking a bit silly and is always clowning around.

Twinkle

This mischievous unicorn always has a twinkle in its eye as if it knows a secret . . . but don't worry, Twinkle would never tell. Twinkle loves planning surprises for friends and there's never a dull moment with this cheeky unicorn around.

Comet

Comet has traveled all over the world and loves to try new things. This unicorn collects interesting things from the countries it visits and is full of amazing stories. Comet has the power of super speed. If you need this unicorn it'll be there in a flash.

Buttercup

Buttercup likes to hide behind a mane of shiny, yellow hair. It's easy to overlook Buttercup in a field of more outgoing unicorns, but it's worth taking the time to get to know this unicorn. Buttercup's a good listener and will always stand by you.

Indus

Indus is an ancient unicorn who has been everywhere and seen everything. Always full of good advice, this is the unicorn to turn to if you have a problem and don't know what to do.

Cha-Cha

This unicorn absolutely loves to dance. With sparkly shoes and amazing dance outfits, Cha-Cha always turns heads. You'll soon forget your worries when you join Cha-Cha on the dance floor.

Genevieve

Genevieve loves to try out the latest fashions and always looks amazing . . . but it's what's on the inside that makes this unicorn really special. Genevieve has a huge heart and loves to take care of friends.

Peaches

Peaches may look soft and cute, but this is a seriously brave unicorn who will always stand up for you. Peaches isn't afraid of anything. Peaches can disappear and reappear so can be by your side at an instant.

Share Your Secrets

Your unicorn is always there to listen to your secrets — and your unicorn would NEVER tell. Use the space below to confide in your unicorn.

Dear ...., (your unicorn's name)

Love from, ... (your name)

ALWAYS BE YOURSELF, UNLESS YOU

CAN BE A

UNICORN

Would You Rather?

Read each of the magical choices below and
make a decision. Would you rather ...

have the wisdom of an ancient unicorn? ☐ **OR** have the energy of a young unicorn? ☐

be able to make rainbows appear? ☐ **OR** be able to make clouds disappear? ☐

be as kind as the kindest unicorn? ☐ **OR** be as clever as the cleverest unicorn? ☐

meet a unicorn who can rap? ☐ **OR** meet a unicorn who can sing? ☐

beat a unicorn in a running race? ☐ **OR** beat a unicorn in a swimming race? ☐

learn about nothing but unicorns at school? ☐ **OR** be taught your usual lessons by a unicorn? ☐

join a team of unicorns in a game of basketball? ☐ **OR** join a team of unicorns in a game of football? ☐

go for tea in the Land of Unicorns? ☐ **OR** have six unicorns join you for tea at your house? ☐

Would you rather...

have a horse for the rest of your life? ☐ **OR** have a unicorn for a week? ☐

have the power to heal humans? ☐ **OR** have the power to heal animals? ☐

travel back in time to see unicorns in the past? ☐ **OR** travel forward in time to see unicorns in the future? ☐

eat marshmallows for lunch? ☐ **OR** eat candy for dinner? ☐

have a unicorn fancy dress outfit? ☐ **OR** have a unicorn onesie? ☐

have the unicorn's power of super hearing? ☐ **OR** have the unicorn's power of super sight? ☐

have eyes that change color depending on your mood? ☐ **OR** have hair that changes color depending on the weather? ☐

write a book about unicorns? ☐ **OR** have a unicorn write a book about you? ☐

The Eyes Have It

Unicorn eyes are mysterious and magical, just like their horns. Add more detail and color the eyes belonging to the unicorns named below.

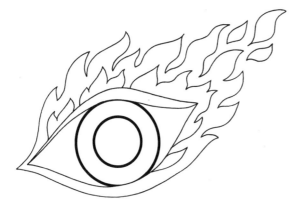

Blaze

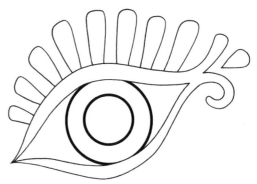

Sunshine

Midnight

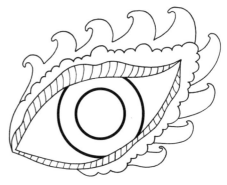

Ocean Storm

Rainbow Burst

Crescent Moon